PERFECT
PRESENTATION

Terry O'Brien is a best-selling author, columnist, consultant and motivational trainer. He is highly sought-after in the corporate as well as academic world, and has been training managers and providing counselling and consultancy over the past couple of decades. Author of hugely popular books on motivation, effective change and all that is 'un-Google-able', his writings focus on skill development and communication techniques. Terry O'Brien is a firm believer that 'infotainment' is a must for content to be effective, and his books are all about the three 'R's: Read, Record and Recall.

OTHER TITLES IN THE SERIES

Perfect Appraisal

Perfect Assertiveness

Perfect Communication

Perfect CV

Perfect Interview

Perfect Leader

Perfect Management Skills

Perfect Marketing

Perfect Meeting

Perfect Negotiation

Perfect People Skills

Perfect Personality

Perfect Salesmanship

Perfect Strategy

Perfect Time Management

PERFECT
PRESENTATION

Get it right every time

Terry O'Brien

RUPA

Published by
Rupa Publications India Pvt. Ltd 2017
7/16, Ansari Road, Daryaganj
New Delhi 110002

Sales centres:
Allahabad Bengaluru Chennai
Hyderabad Jaipur Kathmandu
Kolkata Mumbai

Copyright © Terry O'Brien 2017

The views and opinions expressed in this book are the
author's own and the facts are as reported by him/her which
have been verified to the extent possible, and the publishers
are not in any way liable for the same.

All rights reserved.
No part of this publication may be reproduced, transmitted,
or stored in a retrieval system, in any form or by any means,
electronic, mechanical, photocopying, recording or otherwise,
without the prior permission of the publisher.

ISBN: 978-81-291-4539-0

First impression 2017

10 9 8 7 6 5 4 3 2 1

Printed by Nutech Print Services, New Delhi

Typeset by Chetan Sharma

This book is sold subject to the condition that it shall not,
by way of trade or otherwise, be lent, resold, hired out, or otherwise
circulated, without the publisher's prior consent, in any form of
binding or cover other than that in which it is published.

Contents

	Introduction	*vii*
1.	Making persuasive presentations	1
2.	Tips to handle LCD display projector	5
3.	Handling questions	7
4.	Preparing and delivering presentations	10
5.	Tips for presentations	20
6.	Verbal communication	22
7.	Non-verbal communication	25
8.	Styles of presentation	27
9.	Using cue cards and planning cards	28
10.	Polish your speaking skills	30
11.	The five 'P's of presentation	32
12.	Gear up for public speaking	39
13.	Put yourself across	49
14.	Feedback and cue cards	59
15.	Dos and don'ts	64
16.	Beginning a presentation	68
17.	Concluding a presentation	71
18.	Improve your presentation skills	73

Introduction

Whether your goal is to inform, motivate or inspire, your presentation skills are critical. Effective presenters are made, not born. The *Perfect* series explores important verbal and non-verbal skills, proven presentation structures and innovative delivery techniques that are the hallmarks of impactful presentations.

A presentation is a means of communication that can be adapted to various situations, such as talking to a group, addressing a meeting or briefing a team. A presentation can also be used as a broad term that encompasses other 'speaking engagements', such as getting a point across in a video-conference. To be effective, step-by-step preparation and the method and means of presenting the information should be carefully considered.

A presentation requires you to get a message across to the listeners and will often contain a 'persuasive' element. It may, for example, be a talk about the positive work of your organisation, what you could offer an employer, or why you should receive additional funding for a project. Making a presentation is a way of communicating your thoughts and ideas to an audience.

The role of the presenter is to communicate with the audience and control the presentation.

Presentations are usually delivered directly to an audience. However, there may be occasions where they are delivered from a distance over the internet using video-conferencing systems, such as Skype.

It is also important to remember that if your talk is recorded and posted on the internet, then people may be able to access it for several years. This will mean that your contemporaneous references should be kept to a minimum.

Many factors can influence how effectively your message is communicated to the audience, such as background noise or other distractions, an overly warm or cool room, or the time of day.

As a presenter, you have to be prepared to cope with any such problems and try to keep your audience focused on your message. Here comes a book with tips for you to master this skill, however, the book makes little claim to originality or depth; it is based on the premise of experience and learning.

Indeed, here is all you need to get it right every time!

Making Persuasive Presentations

Be it a new process product or project that a school, industry or organisation should embrace, we should be able to put across a proposal effectively within a limited period of time.

Purpose

Be absolutely clear about your purpose. You should be able to state in one clear sentence what you wish to accomplish. The objective of your presentation may not be the same as the objective of your proposal.

Preparation

- Research your audience (individuals or organisation) thoroughly. What problems or needs do they have related to your proposal? Who are the decision-makers? How open-minded are they likely to be?

- Know exactly how much time you will be given: allocate it for input, audio-visuals and question-and-answer session.
- See the room where you will make the presentation. Where will you stand? Will you need a microphone?
- Have your equipment ready to run: e.g. charts, transparencies and slides checked for proper order; projector, tape recorder and LCD at the desired volume and focus; all preset, tested and adjusted, needing only a 'switch on' to run.

Your introduction needs to grab the audience's attention. It must answer the question: Why should I listen?

Make your listeners identify with you by having thorough knowledge of their situation and needs. Show the gap between what is and what could be. Have a clear structure for your message and repeat it. The organisation of your remarks largely determines how much of your message will be retained.

Possibilities

Name and evaluate the alternative ways of closing the gap between the actual and the ideal.

Proposal

With enthusiasm, show how your proposal meets their needs better than any other possibility. Handle questions pleasantly. Close exactly on time.

How to argue a case

It may be just a debate. It may be a land dispute or a case before a labour court, tribunal or an arbitrator. At any rate, the ability to argue a case effectively is a skill we all can develop. Here are some tips.

- Prepare the case for the other party before you prepare your own. Preparing the strongest possible case for the other party is the best way to anticipate and foresee the other party's strategy and strong points.
- Be sure of your facts.

Problems

- List the facts admitted by both sides; the 'facts' admitted only by one side; and the 'facts' admitted by neither.
- Distinguish clearly the facts and interpretation of facts (conjecture, opinion and hearsay).
- What assumptions are you making? What assumptions may the other party make?
- In legal cases, argue from the definition. The important point is not how we define a term, nor how other people define it, but how the law defines it. The legal definition is crucial and often different from ordinary usage.
- Know the leading cases. Know both those that favour your position and those that don't. Also, what was the precise point of emphasis in each and what was secondary or said only in passing.

- Marshall your arguments. After you have examined the facts, prepared the opposition's case and familiarised yourself with the key definitions and leading cases, you are ready to prepare your own case. What are your strong points and weak points and in what order will you present them?

Speaking Goal

Getting on your feet before an audience always entails a little risk. Take calculated risks, that is, risks that have at least a 50 per cent probability of succeeding. Make sure, however, that there's always a little stretch in your targets.

The ability to put your thoughts across persuasively to groups is a skill that helps in many ways.

Write one speaking goal that you are setting for yourself for the next few months. After writing the goal, assess it for importance and difficulty. Also, check to see whether there is any conflict with any other goal of yours.

Tips To Handle LCD Display Projector

USING LCD PROJECTORS

Read The LCD Projector Manual

Not all LCD projectors work the same way and each has its own unique operating requirements. Familiarise yourself with the projector before using it during the presentation. Make sure your computer can be properly interfaced with the LCD projector.

Practise Setting Up The Equipment Several Times

Spend some time making sure you know how to properly set up the LCD projector with your computer and other computers. Set up the LCD projector in the actual presentation environment you will be using, if possible.

Set Up The Equipment Well In Advance

Allow yourself plenty of time to set up your computer and the LCD projector. Check any last-minute details.

Check The Bulb's Life

LCD projector bulbs have a limited life. Some bulbs have shorter lives than others. Check to make sure the bulb you will be using is not close to the end of its life.

Bring Spare Bulbs And Cables

Always carry spare bulbs with you and make sure you know how to properly change the bulb. Also, remember, 'Hot' glass looks like 'Cold' glass; be careful and bring a towel or glove to use when changing the bulb. Practise changing the bulb during one of your practice sessions.

Check Your Presentation For Colour Combinations

Take some time to check out the presentation for the colour combinations you will be using. Some colours and colour combinations do not project well.

Check The Font Size You Are Using

Nothing is more frustrating to an audience than text that cannot be easily seen or read. Make sure you are using the proper text size for the distance you will be projecting your slides.

Many presentations, today, are followed by a question-and-answer session. For some people, this can be the most exciting part of the presentation. For others, it can be their worst nightmare. In fact, there are some presenters who avoid the question-and-answer session altogether.

Handling Questions

RESPONDING TO QUESTIONS

- Too many people start responding to a question before the entire question has even been asked. Not waiting to hear the entire question can result in you providing a response which has nothing to do with the question. Force yourself to listen to the entire question and make sure you understand it.

- Pause and allow yourself time to value the question and listener. Repeat the question out loud so that the entire audience can hear it. It is important that everyone hears the question or the answer that you provide may not make sense to some of them. Repeating the question, will allow you some additional time to evaluate the question and formulate a response.

- Credit the person for asking the question. You may say something like, 'That was a great question' or 'Glad you asked that question'. A word of caution: If you credit one person with asking a question, be sure to credit everyone who asks a question. You don't want some people to feel that their question was not as important as others'.

- Respond to the question honestly and as best as you can. If you do not know the answer to a question, do not try to fake it. Be honest and tell them you do not know the answer, but do promise to research it for them and do get back to them.

- Bridge the gap to the next question by asking a question. 'Does that answer your question?', 'Is that the kind of information you were looking for?' This is critical. Once they respond to you, with a 'Yes', you can go on to the next person. This also gives them an opportunity to say 'No' and further clarify their question by asking it again.

HANDLING QUESTIONS: ADDITIONAL TIPS

- Ask people to stand up when they ask a question. This does two things. First, you are able to see who is asking the question. Second, it also makes it easier for the audience to hear the question.

- Provide small sheets of paper for people to write down their questions during your presentation, lest they may forget what they were going to ask by the time the question-and-answer session starts.

- Allow people to pass the questions to you, if they feel uncomfortable standing up and asking the question out loud. This gives an option to the person who truly wants to ask a question.

- Always repeat the question. This does three things. First, it ensures that you have understood the question. Second, it gives you a chance to value the question and think of an answer. Third, it ensures that everyone in the audience can hear the question since you are facing them.

- Always think 'before' you answer a question. This allows you time to think, especially for difficult questions. Do the same to questions you readily know the answers for. Responding too quickly to questions you are most comfortable with, will only draw attention to the questions you are not too comfortable with.

- Write down the questions you couldn't answer. This way, you can properly follow-up with the person who asked the question that you couldn't answer. Be sure to get their names and phone numbers or addresses. Promise to get back to them and do get back to them.

Preparing And Delivering Presentations

An effective speaker learns to deal with all seven aspects of preparing and delivering presentations at the same time. Failure to pay attention to a few of these aspects can result in an ineffective presentation. Failure to pay attention to too many of them can result in a disaster.

- Speaker
- Message
- Audience
- Channel
- Feedback
- Noise
- Setting

SPEAKER

One of the major components of any speech or presentation is the speaker himself/herself. Many presenters, today, put so much effort into visual aids that they forget that those are just aids to the speaker.

There are three factors we need to consider about any speaker.
- His/Her motivation in giving the presentation
- His/Her credibility as a speaker
- His/Her delivery or speaking style

Speaker's Motivation

Speaker's motivation can be approached in terms of two considerations.
- Whether direct personal rewards (money) or indirect rewards (feeling good about helping others) are involved.
- Whether immediate rewards (money today) or delayed rewards (getting a college degree after a few years) play a part.

In essence, a speaker may be motivated by one or both of these factors. Before speaking, you should consider what your motivations are.

Speaker's Credibility

A speaker's ideas are accepted as believable only to the degree that the speaker is perceived to be credible. The speaker's credibility depends on his or her trustworthiness, competence and goodwill. The speaker who is well organised will usually be considered competent. The speaker who is attractive and dynamic will be seen as more credible than one who is not.

The most fundamental factor a speaker projects is the attitude he/she has towards himself/herself.

Speaker's Delivery

The delivery, the way the message is presented, should complement the speech's objective. A well-written speech delivered poorly will not be effective.

MESSAGE

The message refers to everything a speaker does or says, both verbally and non-verbally. The verbal part may be analysed in terms of three basic elements.

- Content
- Style
- Structure

Content

This is what you say about your topic. The content is the meat of your speech or presentation. Research your topic thoroughly. Decide on how much to say about each subject. Then decide on the actual sequence you will use. It is important that you consider the audience's needs, time factor and other factors.

Style

The manner in which you present the content of your speech is your style. Styles can vary from very formal to the very informal. Most presentations fall between these two extremes and, for each presentation, the style should be determined by what is appropriate to the speaker, the audience, as well as the occasion and setting.

Structure

The structure of a message is its organisation. There are many organisational variations, but in each case, the structure should include:
- an introduction,
- a body, and
- a conclusion.

The introduction should include:
- an opening 'attention grabber', such as a quote or shocking statistics.
- an agenda.
- the purpose or main message of your presentation.

The body should include:
- the main points or ideas.
- points which support the main message.

The conclusion should include:
- a summary of main points.
- a 'closing grabber'.
- time for question-and-answer session, if required.

When speeches and presentations are poorly organised, the impact of the message is reduced and the audience is less likely to accept the speaker or the speaker's ideas.

AUDIENCE

As a speaker, you should analyse your listeners and then decide how to present your ideas. This analysis might include considerations related to:

- age,
- sex,
- marital status,
- geographic location,
- group membership,
- education, and
- career.

For example, if you are making a presentation on 'Future Careers', knowing your audience's average age is vital. A well-prepared speech that is ill suited to the audience can have the same effect as a poorly prepared speech delivered to the correct audience. Both speeches will fail terribly.

Proper audience analysis will ensure that you give the right speech to the right audience. To properly customise their speech, most professional speakers send their clients a multi-page questionnaire in order to gather relevant information about them.

AUDIENCE As An Acronym

These are the general audience analysis categories that your surveys should include.

Audience: Who are the members? How many people will be attending the event?

Understanding: What is their knowledge about the topic you will be addressing?

Demographics: What is their age, sex, educational background, etc.?

Interest: Why will they be at this event? Who has invited them?

Environment: Where will I stand when I speak? Will everyone be able to see me?

Needs: What are the listeners' needs? What are your needs as a speaker? What are the needs of the person who hired you?

Customised: How can I customise my message to this audience?

Expectations: What do the listeners expect to learn from me?

CHANNEL

When we communicate with our audience, we use many channels of communication. These include non-verbal, pictorial and aural channels.

It is very important that you use as many channels as you can to communicate with your audience. The more channels of communication you can use at the same time, the better. Basically, there are three channels.

Non-verbal
• gestures
• facial expressions
• body movements
• postures

Pictorial
• diagrams
• charts
• graphs
• pictures
• objects

Aural
• tone of your voice
• variations in pitch and volume
• other vocal nuances

FEEDBACK

'Feedback' is the process through which the speaker receives information about how his or her message has been received by the listeners and, in turn, responds to those cues.

The feedback process is not complete until the speaker has responded to the listeners. This process includes the listener's reaction to the speaker's response.

You can ask your audience questions and even ask them what their understanding is of the point you have just made. Watch for non-verbal clues from your audience and be prepared to respond to them throughout your presentation.

It is the speaker's responsibility to provide the information that the audience needs. Many times, you may be asked by the management to provide a specific message to their employees that they may not want to hear. Remember, it is the management that is paying your fee and you are responsible for delivering the message they hired you to deliver. At the same time, it is important that you are sensitive to the audience and try to establish a relationship with them through the use of your surveys, conversations during the social hour and even discussions following your presentation.

PRESENTATION (EVALUATION)

Name: ....

Posture and stance: ....

Clarity and diction: ....

Audibility: ....

Tone and pitch: ....

Eye contact: ....

Facial expressions: ....

Body language: ....

Gestures: ....

Presentation: ....

Three 'V' Assessment

Verbal: ....

Visual: ....

Other remarks: ....

NOISE

There are various noises that a speaker must contend with.
- External noise
- Internal noise

External noise: This consists of sounds—people talking or coughing, poor acoustics, temperature (too warm, too cold), poor ventilation and visual interference including poor lighting or an obstructed view.

Internal noise: If a speaker is confused or unclear about what he or she wants to express, this is due to internal noise. Internal noise can also arise if the speaker does not know or does not analyse the audience.

The role of the audience and the speaker is to simultaneously communicate with each other. '**Response-ability**' is the key. It is this transactional nature of speech that makes feedback and attempts to eliminate noise, so important.

Here are a few effective ways by which a speaker can combat noise.

- Use more than one channel of communication at the same time (verbal and non-verbal).
- Use repetition and restatement.

The speaker can combat internal noise by making an extra effort to use as many channels of communication as possible at the same time. It is important to include both verbal and non-verbal means of communication.

SETTING

The place in which you deliver your presentation may be one that enhances or interferes with the effectiveness of your presentation. Determine ahead of time what the facilities are like before you speak. This way you can properly plan your delivery or make adjustments, if necessary.

Making Effective PowerPoint Presentations

- Use the slide master feature to create a consistent and simple design template.
- Simplify and limit the number of words on each screen.
- Limit punctuation and avoid putting words in all capital letters.
- Use contrasting colours for text and background.

Setting An Objective Is Most Important

Setting an objective for your presentation involves answering three important questions. They are 'who', 'what' and 'why'.

- **Who**–Who are these people?
- **What**–What is the action they should take?
- **Why**–Why will they take this action? What is in store for them?

Tips For Presentations

FOLLOW CONVENTION

People attend conferences to be briefed on topics which they need to know about. They have busy lives and want to leave the conference knowing something new. They want to hear an expert talk about their area of expertise—calmly, authoritatively and factually. The main rule of public speaking is: stand up, speak up and shut up. Be interesting, be clever and be engaging, but if the organiser asks for twenty minutes on the future of 'peer pressure and cyber pressure', it's because that's what he has told the delegates they will get and it's what the delegates have paid their fee. Some speakers try to be funny, unconventional or quirky, and it usually doesn't work. Keep it simple, follow the rules and give the audience what they demand.

Remember, KISS: **K**eep **I**t **S**hort and **S**imple.

AGREE TO THE TERMS OF REFERENCE

Usually, a conference organiser will invite you to speak on a general topic and you'll mutually agree to the points you'll cover. If you commit to covering those points, then cover them.

SPEAKING ALONGSIDE A FAMOUS PERSON

Conference organisers like to invite a famous person to give a keynote speech because it's a good hook to get people to attend their event. You might be lucky—you may be the famous person; if so, well done. But it's more likely that you'll be on the agenda alongside a government minister, an international expert or a media celebrity. Think carefully if you're scheduled to speak before or after the 'star.' While you may be able to bask in reflected glory, they do have a tendency to overshadow other speakers and possibly the event as a whole. Some good speakers lose the attention of their audience when the celebrity arrives in the middle of their speech and all eyes turn away from the speaker and towards that person.

ASSERT YOURSELF

You've been invited to speak at a conference because someone thinks you've something interesting to say, which the delegates should hear. You've got to explain to them why your opinion on the topic is—the one they should pay attention to. Outline briefly and the audience will pay attention. Plan your speech to tell them something they didn't know or wouldn't know by reading research papers.

Verbal Communication

- Material—should be concise, to the point and tell an interesting story (visual aids)
- Voice—how you say—what you say
- Body language—expresses your attitude and thoughts
- Appearance
- Practice is essential

Three 'V's:

Visual

Vocal

Verbal

PREPARATION

- Prepare the structure of the talk carefully and logically
- List the objectives of the talk
- Write out the presentation's matter in rough
- Never read from a script—prepare cue cards – postcards
- Synchronise points with visual aids
- Rehearse your presentation

MAKING THE PRESENTATION

- Greet the audience.
- Keep to the time allocated. It is better to under-run than over-run.
- Don't keep yourself glued to a thought on the screen for too long.
- Stick to the plan.
- Conclude by inviting questions.

INTRO As An Acronym

Interest: Begin with an attempt to make your subject interesting.

Need: Show your listeners why they need to listen.

Title: Make your topic/title absolutely clear.

Rating: Show the area that you plan to cover.

Objective: Your objective or focus on the topic should shine throughout.

DELIVERY

- Speak clearly—judge the acoustics of the room
- Don't rush or talk deliberately slowly—Be natural, although not conversational
- Deliberately pause at key points
- Avoid jokes
- Change pitch of voice
- Look at the audience as much as possible
- Avoid moving about too much and covering the screen
- Keep an eye on the body language of the audience

EMPHASIS

- **Work by contrast principle:** emphasis changes meaning, implies contrast
- **Text devices:** italics, underline, bold, size (font), punctuation, uppercase, colour
- **Headings:** emphasis on key points—be careful of 'u-m-m's and 'e-r-r's.

Non-Verbal Communication

What You Say

- Facial
- Voice paralanguage
- Hand gestures
- Body movements (kinesis)
- Touch
- Personal space

Categories And Features: Broad Categories

- Physical
- Aesthetics
- Signs
- Symbols
- Static features
- Distance
- Orientation

- Posture
- Dynamic features
- Facial expressions

Improve Non-verbal Presentation In Six Ways

- Eye contact
- Facial expressions
- Gestures
- Posture and body orientation
- Proximity
- Paralinguistics (tone, pitch, rhythm, timbre, loudness and inflection)

Styles Of Presentation

The three presentation styles:
- Memorise the presentation
- Write a full script and read from it
- Cue cards—keep short notes by using planning cards

If you memorise, you:
- waste time and effort.
- have to concentrate—the style can become stilted.

Reading from a fully scripted presentation invariably leads to a dull and boring monologue. It is also likely to reduce eye contact and general spontaneity with a resultant loss of impact.

These problems can generally only be overcome by employing a professional speech writer to write the presentation and a professional actor to deliver it.

The use of natural conversational language assisted by pre-prepared cues is almost always the best style for a business presentation. It will help you to sound normal, natural and spontaneous. It will also create a less formal and more relaxed relationship between you and your audience.

Using Cue Cards And Planning Cards

Placing the facts and information, that you have collated, in the correct place within your presentation (structure) is a critical process. Speech-aided cue cards are one of the best ways to put the facts into their effective sequence to support your ideas. Write each fact and piece of information on a separate planning card—these are typically the size of a small postcard. Then by shuffling the sequence of points around, you will be able to experiment until you find the right sequence of points that will have the best effect.

During this process, you may decide to make alterations to your original structure, changing the sequence and relationship between certain messages. Remember that it is the impact and clarity of the messages that is important and not sticking rigidly to a structure that can be improved.

You may also find that certain facts and information are more effective in supporting an alternative message to the one which you had originally envisaged—if that is the case, move the facts. Remember that the rule of thumb when screening your research information is to stop adding facts when your point is clear and present them in order of importance.

Using Cue Cards

At this time, you should have a clear picture of your presentation. You will know the overall message—that is, the aim statement. You will have devised a series of key points and the messages and sub-messages—organised in order of importance, the facts and information that you are going to use—and these will be clearly numbered. Convert your planning cards to cue cards.

These are common presentation aids and their role is precisely to give a cue to the presenter.

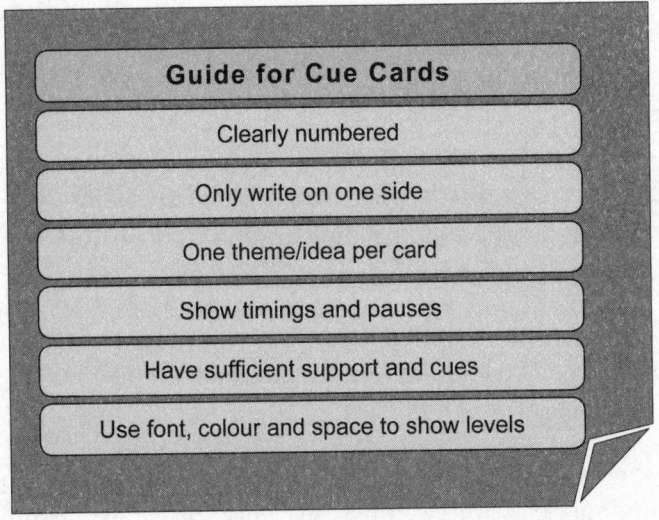

Polish Your Speaking Skills

Many people will do just about anything to avoid public speaking. Or, they may say: 'Who's got the time?' or 'That's not good use of my time.' Therein lies the issue—it's all about time!

The best public speakers make the time to learn about their audience so that what they're saying is what the audience is interested in hearing.

The best public speakers know that timing is everything. They find out exactly what their allotted speaking time is and then practice getting their timing right so they don't over-run or under-run.

The best public speakers appreciate the value of time-out. They leave a 'cushion' of time before and after they speak, to reduce stage fright.

On an average, you'll want to practise your presentation aloud at least three times to work on your opening and closing, your non-verbal language and your voice intonation.

The best public speakers are aware that time marches on. While the first thirty-sixty seconds of a presentation seem like hours due to an elevated stress level, the stress subsides as you proceed with your purpose and realise that the audience is there because they need what you have to offer.

Finally, there's no time like the present to work on your public speaking. Every time you speak, it's a form of public speaking.

Remember: Stand up, speak up and shut up.

The Five 'P's Of Presentation

The Five 'P's Of A Poised And Perfect Presentation

- Planning
- Preparing
- Practising
- Previewing
- Presenting

PLANNING

Things To Note

- How much time will you have for the actual talk? (Plan on leaving 15-20 per cent of the allocated time slot for questions.)
- What audio-visual equipment will be available?
- What kind of audio-visual aids will be expected (depends on field, site and type of presentation)?
- What is the background of your audience?

- Don't get too technical for a general audience.
- Select or pitch your material to match the interests of the audience.
- What the room might be like (assume the worst)?
- **KISS:** Keep It Short and Simple.
- 'Focus' and 'organisation' are even more critical than in written work.
- Repetition is acceptable; listeners will need reminders of things you've already said.
- Slides must be simple, easy to read and legible from a distance. Use high-contrast text/background (black text on white, white text on blue) and best quality photos.
- Choose colours visible to the colour-blind.
- Use a consistent design—same background, same colour or symbol/treatment—throughout.
- Minimise text and set it as bulleted/highlighted statements in 24 points or larger in an easy-to-read font.
- Design the slide to project to the centre of the screen. (Many screens are too small to show very tall or very wide slides.)
- Tables and figures should illustrate a few points only; you might build a complex figure—one curve at a time in a series of slides, until you have all the curves on one graph, or present several short tables—followed by a summary table.
- Figures, especially, may have headings on top that would not appear in a written publication.

PREPARING

In Advance

- Set up slides in a slide tray; mark the number on top right-hand corner; and lock slides in. (Bring your own tray, if possible.)
- Bring a laser pointer, a small battery-operated light, and a timekeeper with large numbers.
- Make large-print note cards/sheets and/or full-size originals of slides.
- Videotape and critique yourself.
- Think about/enact what you might do if a problem arises (projectionist drops and scrambles the slides; projector jams; light blows; power goes out).
- Keep track of time.
- Practice at least once in conditions as close to 'real' as possible.
- Practice out loud.
- Use your slides and notes.
- Use whatever equipment you think you'll have: microphone, projector control and lectern.
- Don't turn the microphone 'On' if you think you may not have one at the venue.
- Have an audience at least once.
- Keep an eye on the audience around the room, especially at the back.
- Ask for a frank critique, including voice quality and volume, distracting mannerisms.

- Ask your audience to come up with questions.
- Preview.
- Check out the room and facilities.
- How will the lights be handled?
- Is there a microphone?
- Who controls the slide projector?
- Is there a lectern?
- Will you be able to see your notes?
- Will the room be dark enough for your slides?
- Preview your slides.

Right Before

- Rest, refuel and relax.
- Prepare mentally for an infinite variety of distractions.
- Remember that you've already come up with solutions to most of the potential problems and you can handle the rest.
- Introduce yourself to the moderator at the earliest opportunity.
- Provide the moderator or host with the material for the introduction, if necessary.
- Give your slides (marked with your name and talk) to the projectionist.
- Lay out what you need (including water) in advance, if you can.

PRACTICING

Why practice? Does practice make perfect?

Practising your speech is essential. So, while practice won't necessarily make you perfect, you will reap significant benefits by practising your speech at least a couple of times.

- Identify awkward phrases and tongue-twisters that you did not notice while writing and editing. Speaking the words out loud exposes flaws that reading does not.
- Gauge your energy level. Does delivering this speech fire you up? Or are you bored with it?
- Gauge your timing. Once you get more experienced, you will learn how many words can fit in a ten-minute time slot. Until then, however, practising the complete speech is the best way to know if you are under or over time.
- Reduce nervousness. Rehearsing, even once, will improve your confidence in your material.
- Recreate the speech setting.
- Practice in the room where you'll be speaking, if you can.
- Stand up for realistic voice projection.
- Rehearse with props and visual aids.
- Arrange an audience.
- Consider what you will wear at the event/presentation.

PREVIEWING

The best way to practise to preview your presentation is by putting it to your computer before having Adobe Connect or a PDF file. Previewing the presentation allows you to see the presentation, listen to the audio, watch video and test quiz questions before launching the presentation in its final format.

Procedure

Begin by opening a PowerPoint presentation. It is a best practice to save Adobe Presenter files to a folder, rather than a location such as your computer's desktop, because multiple files are created during the publishing process. It is recommended that you create a new folder for each presentation that is published to your computer.

PRESENTING

- Convey the excitement and promise of your work.
- Talk to the audience.
- Establish eye contact with various members.
- Watch for the general reaction; adjust as necessary.
- Keep your poise and sense of humour, no matter what.
- Speak distinctly and a little slowly than usual (especially with a microphone).
- Move around casually, if possible.
- Watch out for nervous mannerisms (including speech mannerisms, sighing or pacing).

- If you move, don't get out of range of the microphone or block the screen.
- Use your slides and notes as cue cards.
- Sound as conversational as possible.
- Don't read the talk. (If you must read, make it sound like you're not reading and maintain frequent eye contact with the audience.)
- Deal with questions calmly and with enthusiasm.
- Ask the questioner to repeat the question, if necessary, or you repeat the question as you understand it.
- You are allowed a few seconds to think.
- If you don't know the answer to a question, you could say 'I don't know' or 'it's unknown' (if you know that's so).

Some possible responses (put together as appropriate; use with discretion)

- That's a very interesting/good question…
- I'm glad you asked that…
- We considered that, but didn't do it because…
- I didn't have time to discuss that, but (bit of detail)…
- We're working on that (bit of detail)…
- We'd like to look at that…
- We've applied for funding…
- That's extremely interesting, but…
- It's outside the focus of our research effort…
- Like all methods, this has its limitations; we used it because…

Gear Up
For Public Speaking

KEY PRINCIPLES

Speaking In Public Is Not Stressful

Public speaking is not stressful. Thousands of human beings have learned to speak in front of groups with little or no stress at all. Many of these people were initially terrified to speak in public. Their knees would shake, their voices would tremble and their thoughts would become jumbled. Yet they learned to overcome their fear of public speaking completely.

If they can conquer the fear of public speaking, so can you! It just takes the right guiding principles, the right understanding and the right plan of action to make this goal a reality.

It's not difficult.

You Don't Have To Be Brilliant Or Perfect To Succeed

You don't have to be brilliant, witty or perfect to succeed. That is not what public speaking is all about. You can be average. You can be below average. You can make mistakes, get tongue-tied, or forget whole segments of your talk. You can even tell no jokes at all and still be successful.

It all depends on how you, and your audience, define 'success'. Your audience doesn't expect perfection.

The essence of public speaking is this: give your audience something of value. That's all there is to it. If people in the audience walk away with something or anything of value, they will consider you a success. If they walk away feeling better about themselves, feeling better about some job they have to do, they will consider you a success. If they walk away feeling happy or entertained, they will consider their time with you worthwhile.

Even if you pass out, get tongue-tied or say something stupid during your talk, they won't care! As long as they get something of value, they will be thankful.

They don't even need to feel good to consider you a success. If you criticise people or if you stir them up to ultimately benefit them, they might still appreciate you even though you didn't make them feel good.

All You Need Is Two Or Three Main Points

You don't have to deliver heaps of facts or details. While you may choose to include lots of facts and information, you only need to make two or three main points to make your talk successful. You can even have one key point in your whole talk.

You Also Need A Purpose That Is Right For The Task

This principle is very important. One big mistake people make, when they speak in public, is they have the wrong purpose in mind. Often, they have no specific purpose in mind; this causes a whole lot of unnecessary stress and anxiety. This is what is termed as 'hidden cause' of public speaking stress.

You may be good but someone is going to disapprove of either you or your argument. That is just human nature. In a large group of people, there will always be diverse opinions, judgements and reactions. Some will be positive, others will be negative.

The essence of public speaking is to give your audience something of value. The essence here is *give* not *get*! The purpose of public speaking is not for you to get something (approval, fame, respect and clients) from your audience. It is to give something useful to them.

If you focus on giving as much as you can to your audience, you will then be aligned with the essence of public speaking. You also will avoid one of the biggest pitfalls that cause people to experience public speaking anxiety.

The Best Way To Succeed Is Not To Consider Yourself A Public Speaker

The best way to succeed as a public speaker is not to consider yourself as a public speaker at all.

We often assume that to be successful, we must strive very hard to bring forth certain idealistic qualities that we do not possess.

The problem is that we try to become someone other than

ourselves. We try to be a public speaker, whatever that image means to us.

The truth about public speaking is that most successful speakers became successful by being themselves. They didn't try to be somebody else. Sincerity and authenticity is the bottom line of public speaking, in fact, in any type of communication. When people are just themselves in front of other people, it is then that they discover how much fun they can have doing something most other people dread.

Don't try to become public speakers! No matter what type of person we are, or what skills and talents we possess, we can stand up in front of others and fully be ourselves.

In public speaking, we can fully be ourselves in the presence of others. One can be bold, compassionate, silly, informative, helpful, witty or anything one wants. One can tell jokes, tell humorous or poignant anecdotes, or do anything else that feels natural in the moment.

The speaker is alive; the speaker is geared up. He is fully invested in everything he says and does. That's another gift a speaker can give to his audience. It also allows him to tell when he has gone on too long or when the attention of the people, who are listening to him, begins to stray away.

Sometimes, we enjoy throwing ourselves in front of a group without knowing specifically what we're going to say. The speaker could just focus on the main points and remember that he is there to give people something of value. In many instances, he will say things he's never said before! They just come out of him spontaneously while 'being with his audience'.

Don't try to give talks the way someone else does. Just go out there, armed with a little knowledge and a few key points, and be yourself. Everything else will usually work out.

Humility And Humour

Humility and humour can go a long way in making your talks more enjoyable and entertaining for your audience.

If you are comfortable with being humorous, or if it fits your speaking situation, go for it. It usually works, even if you don't do it perfectly.

Humility means standing up in front of others and sharing some of your own human frailties, weaknesses and mistakes. We all have weaknesses; when you stand up in front of others and show that you're not afraid to admit yours, you create a safe, intimate climate where others can acknowledge their personal shortcomings as well.

But beware; don't begin your talk with the cliché: 'I couldn't prepare this talk as I was busy, but I will talk on…' This will be a confession that you are here to waste time.

Being humble in front of others makes you more credible, more believable and paradoxically more respected. People can connect with you more easily. You become 'one of them'. It also sets a tone of honesty and self-acceptance. True humility is easily distinguished from the pretence of acting humble. If you pretend, your audience will perceive this and lose respect for you.

Humour and humility can be combined very effectively. Telling humorous stories about yourself, or using your own personal failings to demonstrate a point that you are trying to make can be both entertaining and illuminating.

If you get nervous when you stand up to speak in front of a group, don't hide this fact from your audience. Be real and humble; acknowledge your fears openly and honestly.

You can start your talk with a humorous story that produces the same effect. Try wit also: 'tough reasonableness'. This is an intellectual quality. Humour has an undercurrent of feeling.

Believe: When You Speak In Public, Nothing 'Bad' Can Ever Happen!

What if they all get up and leave after the first ten minutes? What if they put up harsh questions or comments once I'm done? What if someone in the audience tries to turn the group against me?

Most of these things don't happen. Just in case they do, it's useful to have a strategy in mind.

Most of the 'negative' things that happen when one is speaking can be handled by keeping one principle in mind—everything that happens can be used to one's advantage.

If people get up and start to head for the door, I can stop what I'm doing and ask for feedback.

- Was there something about my topic, my style or my manner of presentation that was offensive?
- Were they simply in the wrong room at the start and didn't know it?
- Did someone misinform them about what my talk was going to cover?

Even if everyone walked out and refused to give a reason, one could ultimately find ways to benefit from this experience.

You Don't Have To Control The Behaviour Of Your Audience

To succeed as a public speaker, you don't have to control the behaviour of your audience. You do, however, need to control your own thoughts, preparation, arrangement for audio-visual aids, and how the room is laid out. But the one thing you don't have to control is your audience.

If people are restless, don't try to control them. If someone is talking to a person next to him, or reading the newspaper, or has fallen asleep, leave them alone. If people look like they aren't paying attention, refrain from criticising them.

In General, The More You Prepare, The Worse You Might Do

Preparation is useful for any public appearance.

If you have the wrong focus (i.e. purpose), if you try to do too much, if you want everyone to applaud your every word, if you fear something bad might happen or you might make a minor mistake, then you can create stress for yourself. In this case, the more effort you put in, the worse you will probably do.

Remember, if you know your subject well, or if you've spoken about it many times before, you may only need a few minutes to prepare sufficiently. All you might need is to remind yourself of the two or three key points you want to make.

Over-preparation usually means you don't feel confident about your ability to speak in public. You'll need to develop trust in your natural ability to speak successfully. Solicit opportunities to speak on your subject in public. If you have something of value to tell others, keep getting in front of people and deliver it. In no time at all, you'll gain confidence.

Your Audience Truly Wants You To Succeed

The last principle to remember is that your audience truly wants you to succeed. Most of them are scared of public speaking, just like you. They know the risk of embarrassment, humiliation and failure that people take every time they present themselves in public. So they will feel for you. They will admire your courage. The audience will be on your side, no matter what happens.

> **Hidden Causes Of Public Speaking Stress**
> - Thinking that public speaking is stressful (it's not).
> - Thinking you need to be brilliant or perfect to succeed (you don't).
> - Trying to impart too much information or cover too many points in a short presentation.
> - Having the wrong purpose in mind.
> - Trying to please everyone (this is unrealistic).
> - Trying to emulate other speakers (very difficult) rather than simply being your true self (very easy).
> - Failing to be frank and upfront.

- Being fearful of potential negative outcomes.
- Trying to control the wrong things, such as the behaviour of your audience.
- Spending too much time over preparing (instead of developing confidence and trust in your natural ability to succeed).
- Thinking your audience will be as critical of your performance as you might be.

Key Principles To Always Keep In Mind
- Speaking in public is not stressful.
- You don't have to be brilliant or perfect to succeed.
- All you need is two or three main points.
- You also need a purpose that is right for the task.
- The best way to succeed is not to consider yourself a public speaker.
- Humility and humour can go a long way.
- When you speak in public, nothing 'bad' can ever happen!
- You don't have to control the behaviour of your audience.
- In general, the more you prepare, the worse you might do.
- Your audience truly wants you to succeed.

Dos and don'ts in public speaking

Dos	Don'ts
Prepare your speech	Don't read out your speech or learn your speech by heart
Practice	Don't apologise
Relax	Don't use slides with too much information
Start your speech with a punch-line	Don't fall in love with the sound of your voice
Say it like you mean it	Don't lean while speaking; maintain eye contact

Put Yourself Across

I keep six honest serving men (they taught me all I knew). Their names are: 'What', 'Why', 'When', 'How', 'Where' and 'Who'.

WHAT AND WHY

Deciding The Objective

General Objectives	Specific Objectives
To persuade or sell	These depend on the subject matter entirely
To teach	
To stimulate thought	
To inform	
To entertain*	

*Whatever be your general objective, there is always a need to entertain your audience.

This does not mean cracking jokes. It means that the material must be put across in such a way that it is interesting and people want to listen.

Note: It is an excellent idea to write down the objective of the speech in one sentence. This has various benefits.

- It clears the speaker's mind right at the start.
- When your notes are complete, you can check that you are meeting your original aim.

WHO

Researching The Audience

Audience is the most important in the whole exercise.

What should you know about audience?

- How many persons are there?
- Why are they there? Are they there of their own free will? Were they sent to listen? Are they paying?
- What is their present knowledge of the subject of the talk?
- Are they likely to have any bias towards or against the subject or the speaker?
- What are their expectations from the talk and the speaker?
- What age, range and sex are they?

The bottom line is 'response-ability'.

WHERE

Preparing The Environment

It is important to consider where the talk is going to take place. The size of the room must be aligned with the pitch of your voice.

HOW

How Things In The Room Work

Become aware of:
- any likely distractions for you and your audience.
- the possibility of noise/general interruption.

Pitch your speech at the right level: A woman talking to a group of men about women's equality would be different when talking to a group of women. Similarly, a computer expert will talk differently with experts and novices.

WHEN

Timing

- **Time of the day:** After lunch session is known as the 'Graveyard' session in training circles.
- **How long does one get:** Keep to time.
- **Right amount of material for the talk:** If there is no clock in the room, take off your watch and put it on the podium.

SEATING

Theatre Style

Formal atmosphere and eye contact with the audience is more difficult to achieve.

Horse-shoe

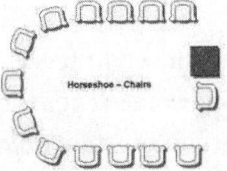

Single row of people seated in a horse-shoe shape is informal and conducive to participation.

Curved

Similar problems as with the theatre style but slightly less formal.

Cabaret Rows

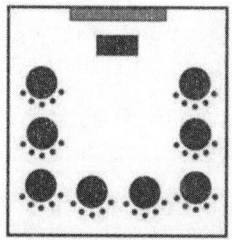

People sitting in groups around tables; it is useful if you break the audience into formal discussion groups.

Points to watch

- Most people have a tendency of having too many chairs. Rope off the back rows.
- Ideally, you want the audience as close to you as possible.
- Try to make sure the seats are not too comfortable. Low, soft chairs can be sleep inducing—the last thing you want from the audience.
- The environment you have can either hinder or help. The aim is to minimise the hindrances and maximise the good points.

GENERAL PREPARATION

- Why am I speaking?
  Clarify the objective.
- Whom am I speaking to?
  Research the audience.
- Where am I speaking?

> Familiarise yourself with the venue and equipment. Anticipate distractions and arrange the seating suitably.
>
> - When am I speaking? At what time of the day? How long have I got?
>
> Anticipate lack of concentration.

PREPARING THE MATERIAL

A speech will almost certainly fail unless careful thought is given to the subject matter.

The following stages of preparation will help your thought process in the preparation of the material and ensure that your speech is well-structured and lively.

Structuring Your Talk

- It is essential to write all thoughts and ideas on your subject on a paper. Making pattern notes might be useful.
- Take a plain sheet of paper. Write the objectives of your talk at the top and the main 'terms' of your talk in the centre of the page in a circle.
- Write down all the ideas and thoughts you have on the subject, starting from the circle and branching out along lines of connecting ideas.
- Let your mind be as free as possible. Do not restrict your thoughts by deciding where each point should go in a list. Your ideas should flow easily.

- When finished, circle any related ideas and sections and establish your order of priorities and organisation.

COMPLETED PATTERN NOTE

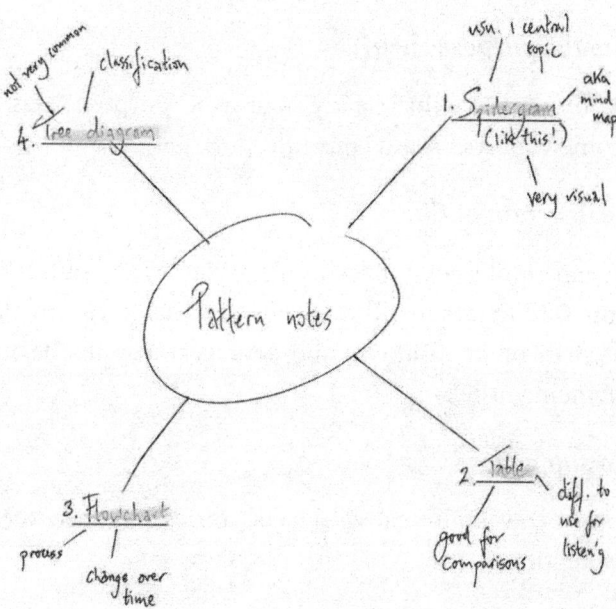

Steps To Preparation

Purpose of the speech

Is the purpose of your talk to inform, to persuade, to entertain, or to call your audience to action? Every speech must have its own being.

Analyse the audience

Speak what the audience knows and cares for.

Gather enough material

Start collecting your thoughts and notes. After you have exploited your thoughts, go to the library, ask colleagues and research. Research gives you a reserve that you draw on.

State the purpose clearly

Frame a sentence that clearly states your purpose. This will become your focus and your title.

Construct an outline

You can't build your speech unless you lay its foundation. In the outlines, you will reduce your ideas to two or three sentences or key phrases and arrange them in the most convincing order.

Add support

Support your argument with facts, stories and anecdotes to give depth.

Prepare the visuals

If used properly, visual aids can be effective.

Devise an opening with an impact

You make your first impression in the opening. The opening may be humorous, surprising, informative or challenging—an opening can be anything original that works for a particular speech.

Craft your conclusion

Build up to it, even if you are ending by summarising your main points.

Write, polish and edit

Edit ruthlessly. Don't be afraid to cut one-third or even one-half of your prose. This will leave you with a script that is stronger, leaner and cleaner. Effective written communication is different from its oral counterpart. A speech is a temporary event—words float in the air and are gone. Your words will have a better chance of staying with your audience if you take advantage of oral communication's greater informality.

Prepare confidence cards

Check if they are numbered. So that if you drop them, you can get them back in order.

Get your timing down

Part of practising your speech is timing your speech. We speak approximately 150 words in a minute. So three double-spaced typewritten pages will be read in about five minutes, depending on how quickly you speak.

Make a last-minute checklist

A key aspect of preparation is controlling your speaking environment.

Before your speak:
- make two copies of your text or notes.
- bring your glasses.
- know if you'll have a podium.
- prepare visual-aid and equipment.
- Think: Have I orchestrated the question-and-answer session?
- Think: What is the purpose behind this speech?
  - Who is the audience and what is its main interest in this topic?
  - What are the main points of my outline?
  - What visual aids do I need?
  - Do I have an arresting opening?
  - Have I polished and practised the language of the speech?
  - Have I taken care of all little details?
- decide what you are going to wear.

Feedback And Cue Cards

CUE CARDS

Using Cue Cards Effectively

Making cue cards from standard office supply index or note cards is relatively easy. Using them well will lift the quality of your presentation immeasurably.

This will enable you from not relying on and reading text word-for-word. You are free to interact with your audience. Further, you are able to make eye contact, respond, make gestures and move freely. You will sound, look and feel more present—'in the moment'. Your entire delivery is enlivened. For those of you, who are nervous about making the transition from a full script to note cards, don't be. Take it slowly. Take time to thoroughly rehearse. You'll be effective and confident.

Making Cue Cards

Use a collection of different coloured highlighters.

You need:

- a packet of standard index cards,
- a few highlighters (for example: yellow, pink, blue and green), and
- an easily-read pen. (Preferably use one with either blue or black ink.)

The Best (Most Useful) Cue Cards

These cards ought to have one main heading or idea per card written clearly using larger than usual font (so you can read them easily). Also, have plenty of white space around each word or phrase to help them stand out. Use bullet points or numbers to write supporting ideas under the main heading. Write on one side of the card only. If clearly numbered, you will know the order they come in and/or they may even be tied together. (Drill a hole through the left corner and tie with a loop of string so that the cards can be flipped.) Have a colour-coded theme to show your main idea, supporting ideas, examples and transitions or links. For example: Main Idea One → Supporting Idea → Example → Show slide 1. Have approximate timings marked so you can track yourself through your allotted time. If you find you're going over, you can adjust by leaving out an extra example or, conversely, if you're under time, you can add one in.

Preparing The Speech For Cue Cards

Before starting on the cue cards, make sure you've got the flow of the speech how you want it. Using your speech outline, from the beginning, check the sequence of ideas, supporting material and their transition to ensure that all your information is recorded/structured in an effective and logical sequence. Do try it out loud and time it. You may need to edit it, if it's too long, and it's a lot easier to do that at this stage.

Is Your Speech Being Evaluated?

If your speech is being judged, find out what the evaluator will be marking you on. Check a standard speech evaluation form.

Once you have the length right for your time allowance, if possible, get other people to listen to you. Have them give you feedback on content, structure and delivery; pay attention to the introduction and the conclusion. When you're satisfied, you have your speech as you want it, you're ready to prepare cue cards.

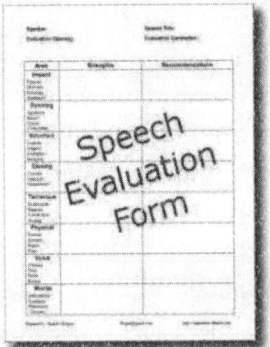

Writing Cue Cards

Each segment of your speech, from its introduction to conclusion, should be reducible to a key word or phrase that will act as a prompt, triggering your memory for what it was that you wanted to say. Go through your outline marking each of them. A good way to identify them is to remember the paragraph structure that you use in written prose. A new thought or idea takes a new paragraph. In writing note cards, a new idea or thought equals a new card.

Using An Android App

If you'd rather use your Android device, there are very simple apps allowing you to create cards with titles and notes.

Do not be tempted to write the whole of the text of your speech out. This defeats your purpose. You'll finish with cramped notes that stop you from freely interacting with your audience and are difficult to read.

Once you've finished identifying segments and giving each a keyword or phrase, you're ready to write your cards using the guidelines above.

Decide on the colour coding you're going to use, such as pink for main ideas, blue for supporting ones, yellow for quotes and important facts and green for transition. The final take of colours is yours.

Number each card in the same place. The top right hand corner works well for most. Write, as a heading in the top left, which part of the card is meant for introduction, body and conclusion. It helps you to keep track of where you are.

Double check the effectiveness of each card as you write them to make sure you are using keywords or phrases that actually do trigger your memory. This is particularly important for links or transitions. Forgetting how you got from one piece of information to the next, leaves both you and your audience stranded.

Be sure to note the names of important people, facts or processes.

Feedback Form

Name:		Date:		
Please answer these questions truthfully. Tick your answers in the 'Yes' or 'No' columns.			Yes	No
1.	Were the objectives of the programme clear?			
2.	Do you agree that the correct topics were targeted?			
3.	Did the programme meet your expectations?			
4.	Did the programme hold your interest throughout?			
5.	Was the information presented in a proper manner/logical sequence?			
6.	Was the information presented clearly? Did you understand what was taught to you during the training?			
7.	Was the content of the course relevant?			
8.	Did the examples/illustrations help you to learn?			
9.	Did the practice exercises/activities help you to learn?			
10.	Do you feel you have gained valuable knowledge from this programme?			
11.	Were you able to relate with the trainer during the programme?			
12.	Is there any particular area where you require training?			
	Suggestions:			
	General Comments:			

Dos And Don'ts

DOs

- Check what is expected of you when you are invited to speak.
- Give yourself plenty of time to prepare.
- Establish a clear structure.
- Prepare good, summarised notes.
- Realise and accept that all good speakers experience nervous tension before speaking.
- Plan and rehearse the start with care.
- Put pace and enthusiasm into your delivery.
- Ensure you are clearly audible to everyone.
- Maintain good, evenly-distributed eye contact with your audience.
- Plan and rehearse the conclusion with care.

DON'Ts

- Prepare too much material: check your timing.
- Try to do without speaker's notes.
- Read the script verbatim.

- Start with an apology.
- Risk weak or dodgy jokes.
- Split your audience's attention by misuse of aids or handouts.
- Rock, sway or use repetitive gestures.
- Clutter your visual aids.
- Gabble or rush.
- Assume hostility.

PRESENTATION

Dos

Empathise: Always begin a presentation by explaining how your product or service addresses the audience's pain. If you empathise with their concerns and provide a worthwhile solution, you will be more likely to gain customers than forcing your audience to identify with a problem they may not have.

Edit: You could talk about your company forever, but don't. Presentations are meant to educate and intrigue, not to bore. Give your audience enough information to pick their interest and then direct them to other resources for more information.

Minimise word count: If you are using PowerPoint, put no more than ten words on each slide. Minimising text on the slide also minimises distractions, allowing your audience to focus on your speech and your message.

Relate to the audience: Use personal stories, examples and custom demos to help your audience relate to you.

Remember, their problem should be your problem, so don't be shy about letting the audience know you understand their concerns.

Rehearse, rehearse, rehearse: Do not just think you can wing a presentation. You need to rehearse and then warm up. Feeling comfortable and practised will help calm your nerves and keep you from freezing onstage.

Follow-up, stand out: Once the presentation has ended, don't let your communication skills fall flat. Be sure to follow-up with any individuals you met before or after the presentation, and make sure your electronic communication is as effective as your in-person communication.

Don'ts

Try to be funny if you're not: Humour doesn't always translate onstage, particularly if it's not practised. Rather than trying to dress up a presentation with unnecessary elements, focus on delivering an impactful and engaging message, and you will succeed every time.

Focus on a big stunt: Often presentations, especially those where you are pitching your company, are limited to a few short minutes. Don't waste time trying to execute a stunt that has nothing to do with your product or company, spend those precious minutes talking about what you actually have to offer.

Leave your personality backstage: People want to feel a personal connection to your brand. They want to feel like they are doing business with an actual person rather than a company. That human element has to come from you. Showing personality onstage lets the audience see the person behind the company and makes for a more engaging presentation—something every presenter should strive for.

Read your slides: Do not ever do this. Even a well-practised presenter comes off sounding monotonous and boring when reading slides. Plus, breaking eye contact with your audience is a sure-fire way to lose their interest.

Practice, but don't memorise and don't read word-for-word. If you mess up or stumble, that's okay. If anything, it brings out that human element the audience is seeking.

Waste time: People attend presentations with a specific objective in mind: to learn. Don't waste their time by talking about irrelevant information or showcasing unnecessary 'flair'. Being succinct is your responsibility as a presenter and something your audience will thank you for.

Forget to prepare for questions: Often speakers focus on the presentation so intently that they forget to prepare for the question-and-answer session afterwards. Don't be that person. Try to anticipate the kinds of questions they might have and be prepared with answers. A poorly planned question-and-answer session can over-shadow even the most successful presentation.

Presentation etiquette: It all comes down to one thing: valuing your audience. This means speaking directly to them, having all the information prepared and practised, and above all, being worthwhile of their time. If you remain focused on providing value to your audience, you'll find yourself giving successful presentations every time.

Beginning A Presentation

OPENING

Here are a few pointers to help you make an impressive beginning.

- **Greet your audience:** This is the very basic, common and important step in which you need to greet your audience by wishing them good morning/afternoon/evening.

- **Compliment and show gratitude:** After greeting your audience, compliment them and choose some words which show that you are delighted to see them there. For example: 'It's great to see you all' or 'Thank you for coming here, today.'

- **Give your introduction:** Start with telling your audience your full name. You can show some informal attitude by telling them your short/nickname. Then, introduce yourself professionally and give information about what you do and why you are here today.

- **Signpost:** Give all your information to them. Then, present your proposal and related information, as well as key points.

Here is an example.

> Good afternoon everyone. It's great to see you all here. Thank you for coming. My name is Gurcharan Singh, friends call me Garry sometimes. I am a software engineer by profession and working with XYZ Ltd. Today, we are here to know about a new software so that we can make the most of it. First, we will look at how it works; next, we will discuss where can we use it; then, we will learn what are its advantages; and finally, we will discuss what precautions are required while implementing it.'

The purpose of a good introduction in a formal presentation is to achieve three goals.

- Catch the audience's attention.
- Identify the topic and the purpose or core message of the talk.
- Provide a brief overview or agenda of what you will cover in the talk.

Speakers often overlook the part about getting the audience's attention. They just start talking without capturing the interest of the audience. The key point to keep in mind here is that if you don't grab your group's attention from the very outset, you may not have it for the rest of your presentation. The following are some useful opening techniques that gain the audience's attention in a positive way.

- **Quote someone:** When using a quote, you must cite the source and tie up the quotation to your topic.
- **Add humour:** A touch of humour is a great way to break the ice with the audience: As with a quote, the

humorous anecdote must be tied up to the topic you're going to talk about. Otherwise, it serves as a distraction and can turn the audience off regardless of its humour.

- **Share a story:** A *short* story—with the emphasis on short—is another clever way to kick off a presentation. To work, the story needs to make a point or contain a message that is related to the talk that follows.

- **Make a bold statement:** This technique involves a brief, thought-provoking statement that sets up your topic. If you say it with a strong voice, it commands attention and gets the group eager to hear what will follow.

- **Get the audience to participate:** With this technique, you start your presentation by having the audience do something, from a brief exercise to responding to questions. This technique gets people's energy levels up. However, don't choose an activity that creates such a ruckus that getting the audience to focus back on you becomes difficult.

- **Ask a rhetorical question:** A rhetorical question is a thought-provoking question that you ask the audience but don't expect them to answer out loud. When you ask the question, you want to answer it either within your introduction or a short time later in your talk. Otherwise, the question serves only to confuse people.

As you prepare your introduction, carefully plan the opening technique you want to use to grab the audience's attention. Whether you start with this technique or with identifying your topic briefly doesn't matter. Just go with what works for you.

Concluding A Presentation

EFFECTIVE ENDINGS

To be truly effective, take questions and then finish with a closing that is as powerful as the beginning of your presentation.

Here are three techniques for creating a memorable ending.

A Quote

Use a quote that will stay with your audience long after they leave the room.

For example: The best thing about our company is that it gives the best.

A Call To Action

Most business presentations' primary purpose is to move the audience to action. Use the last few minutes of the presentation to reinforce the call to action.

For example:
- Begin the journey
- Improve the process

Assume that your presentation has delivered the information needed by the audience and make your call to action definitive and instructional.

A Compelling Story

Ending your presentation on a story—especially if that story is personal or illustrates how the content presented could affect others—is the best way to conclude.

What you say in the end is what the audience takes back home!

The last thirty seconds matter! You may end with:
- a surprising fact.
- a provocative question. Ending with a question or a rhetorical question, is a sure-fire way to gain attention because questions stimulate our thoughts.
- an unusual quote.
- a touch of humility.
- a powerful visual.
- a parabola. The structure must be a return to your opening.

Improve Your Presentation Skills

- Practice.
- Transform nervous energy into enthusiasm.
- Attend other presentations.
- Arrive early.
- Adjust to your surroundings.
- Meet and greet.
- Use positive visualisation.
- Remember that most audiences are sympathetic.
- Smile.
- Work on your pauses.
- Don't try to cover too much material.
- Actively engage the audience.
- Be entertaining.
- Admit you don't have all the answers.
- Use a powerful stance.

Effective Presentation skills

Structure
Have a logical order: introduction, body with your main points and a conclusion.

Practice
Practice beforehand in front of a mirror, with a recorder or in front of a friend.

Body language
Smile, make eye contact, stand up straight and move around a bit. Don't hide behind the podium!

Notes and handouts
Have brief notes on postcard-sized cards. Have a handout that the audience can take away afterwards.

PowerPoint presentations
Keep slides clean and simple, Don't have lots of text on each slide. Use charts, diagrams and pictures.

Speech
Speak clearly, confidently, and not too fast. Use everyday language rather than jargon.

Interaction
Build a rapport with your audience. Get them involved by asking questions. Use humour, if appropriate.

Nervousness
It's normal to be a bit nervous. Preparation and practice will reduce nervousness!

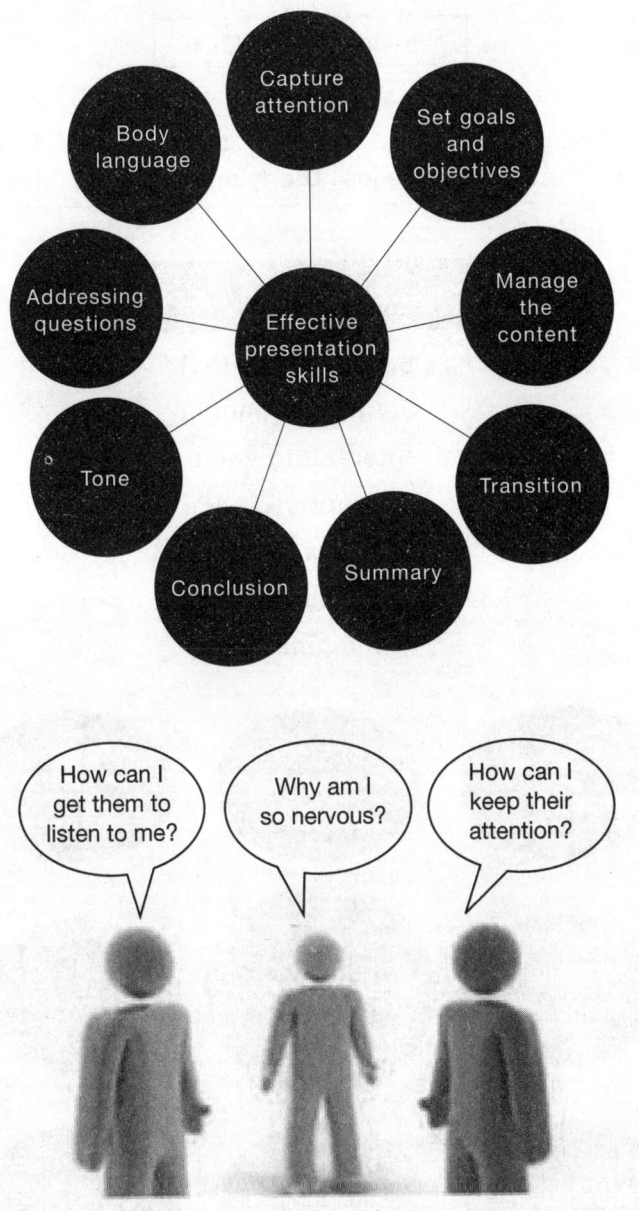

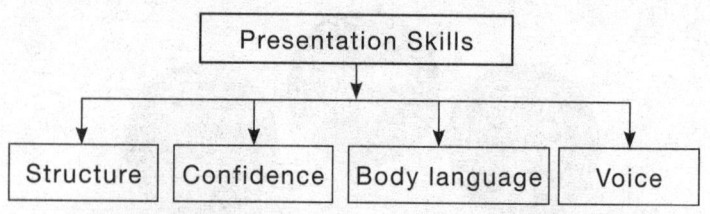

Characteristics of a good presenter

Good eye contact
Confident manner
Interesting voice
Appropriate pace
Knowledge
Enthusiasm
Imagination

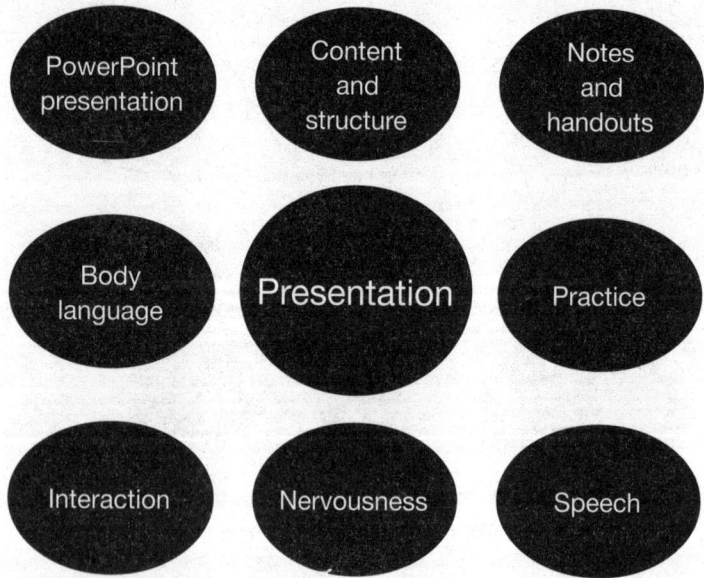

PRESENTATION SKILLS

These steps should be included in preparing an effective presentation.

- Plan
- Prepare
- Practice
- Present

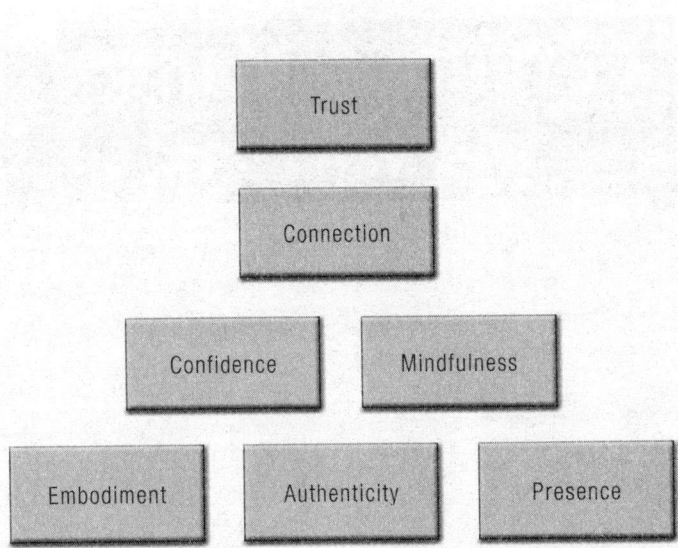

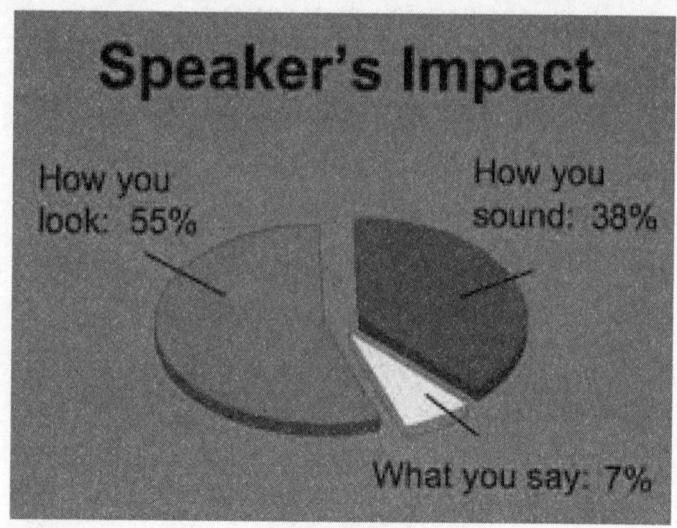

PERFECT APPRAISAL

Performance appraisal is the process of evaluating and documenting one's performance on the job. It is part of career development. This book deals with the appraisal process, training for appraisal, pitfalls in appraisal and the dos and don'ts of appraisal.

Perfect Appraisal provides simple techniques to a perfect appraisal with a holistic approach.

PERFECT ASSERTIVENESS

Assertiveness is important in all forms of communication. It is a way of relating to others that respects both your own and other people's needs, wants and rights. Aggressiveness provokes counter-aggression, assertiveness doesn't. This book spells out assertiveness training, responses—passive, aggressive and assertive, effective communication, assertiveness skills and the benefits of being assertive.

Perfect Assertiveness helps you understand assertiveness as a life skill.

PERFECT COMMUNICATION

Communication is the process of sharing information, knowledge or meaning. What matters most is the 'response-ability'; response is more important than the message. Listeners must not just hear; they must listen. This book deals with speaking skills, writing skills and listening skills.

Perfect Communication is much more than just this.

PERFECT CV

A curriculum vitae (CV) or résumé presents a record of your qualities, skills and experience to an employer, so that your suitability for a particular job can be assessed. In Latin, 'curriculum vitae' means 'the way your life has run' and 'résumé' is the French word for 'summary'. This book deals with making a CV special, writing a CV with lack of experience, tailoring a CV and digital and online CVs.

Perfect CV helps you to compile your CV and suggests ways to improve it.

PERFECT LEADER

If you want to inspire, motivate and engage, and move people into action, leadership is the ability you require. Leaders set direction and develop the skill to guide people to the right destination. This book spells out leadership styles, initiatives that are needed, proactive tools, the importance of perseverance and methods to step out of the comfort zone.

Perfect Leader helps you to inspire the vision of the future as a leader. It equips you to make strategic decisions, shape conflict and find your competitive edge.

PERFECT MEETING

Meetings help one to build rapport. They are a forum for inter-learning and understanding; a platform to share information. *Perfect Meeting* is about the basic skills of management. This book deals with effective meetings, conference meetings, stand-up meetings, one-on-one meetings and the tasks and skills of the chairperson.

Perfect Meeting helps you generate cooperation and commitment to attain higher levels of performance.

PERFECT NEGOTIATION

In order to settle differences, one needs to master the skill of negotiation. Without this skill, conflicts and disagreements will arise. This book deals with the process of negotiation and its different stages: preparation, discussion, goals, win-win outcome and agreement.

Perfect Negotiation helps you master the different types of negotiation formats, styles, and preparing strategies for negotiation.